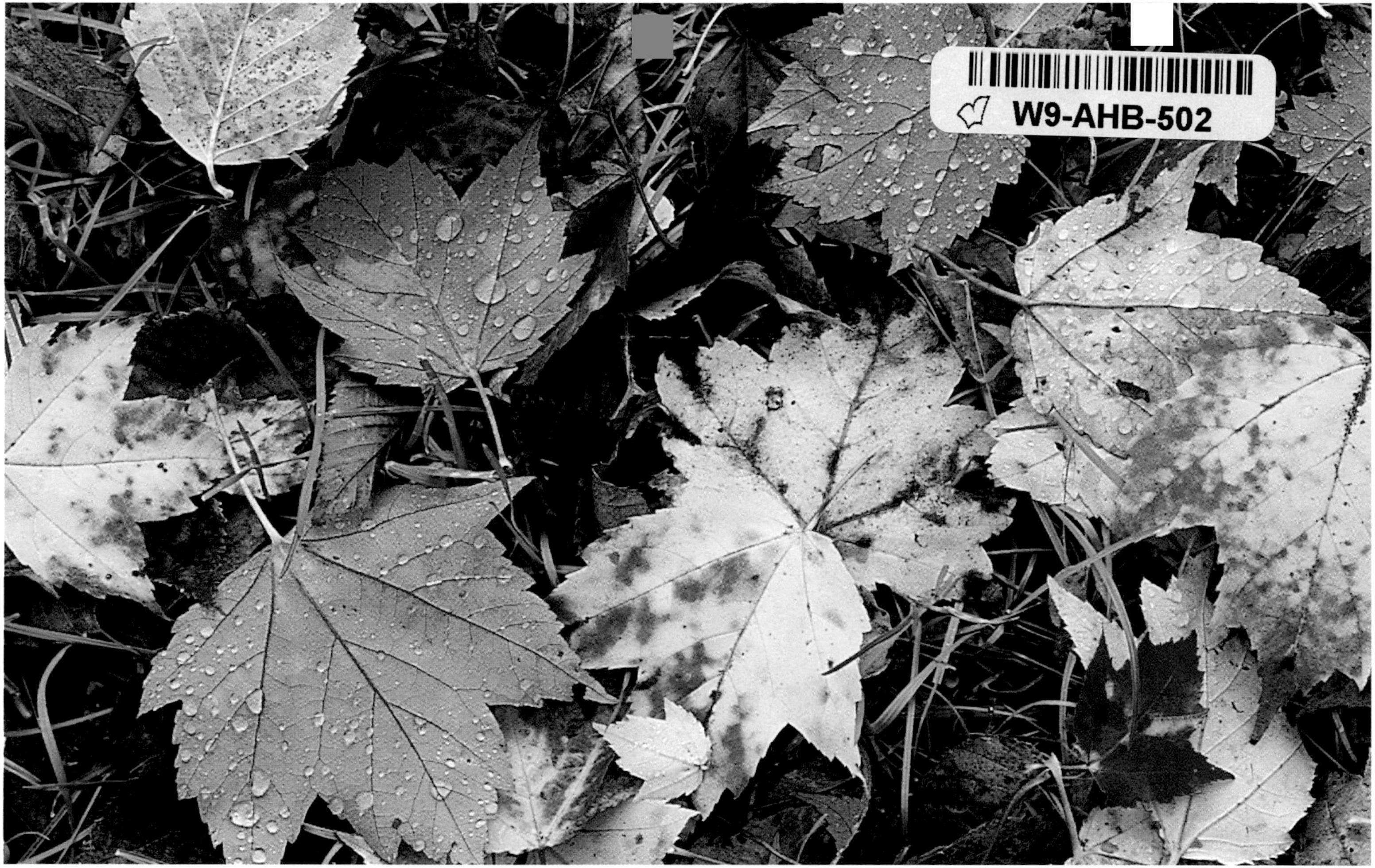

leaves

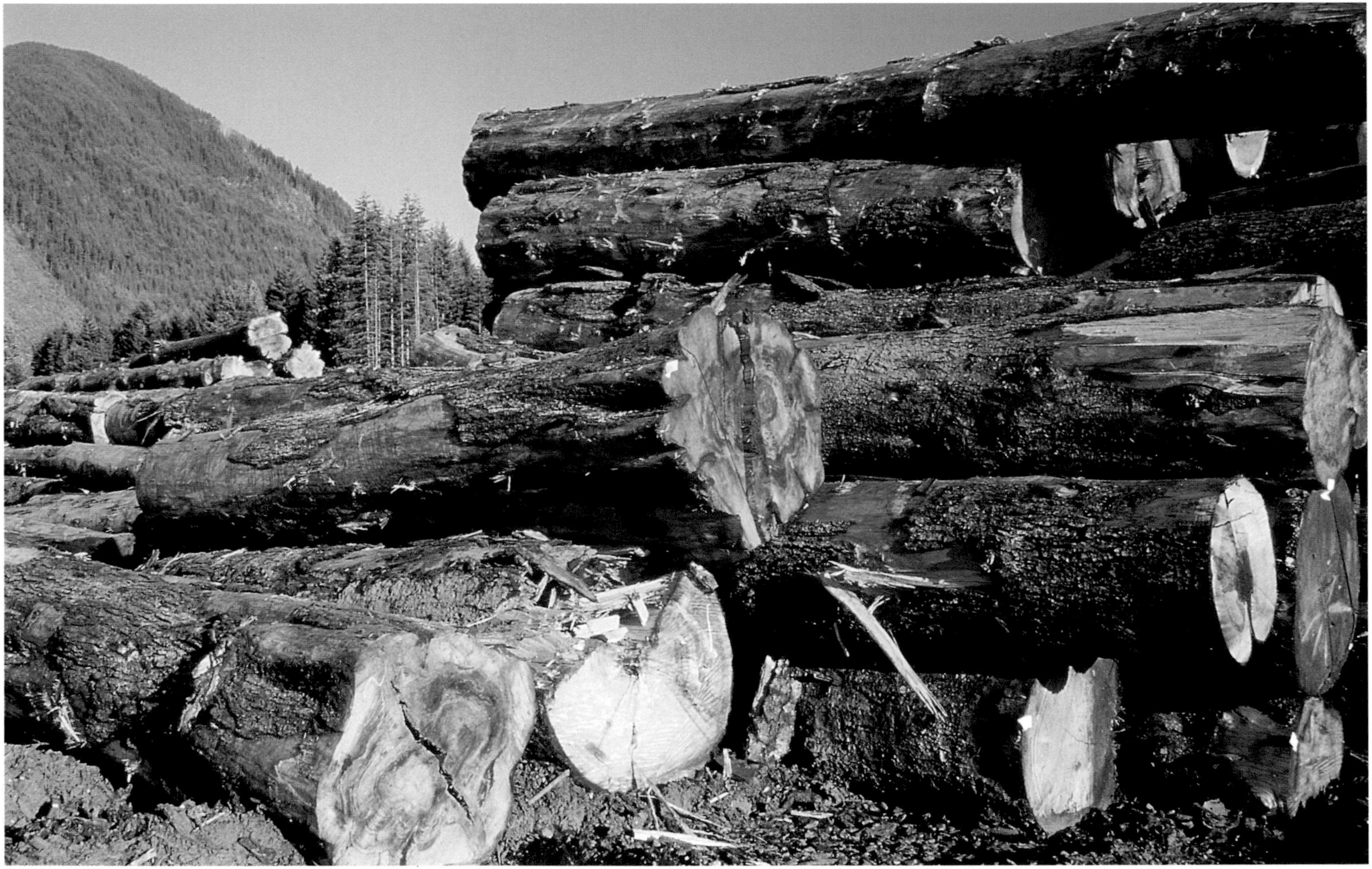

logs

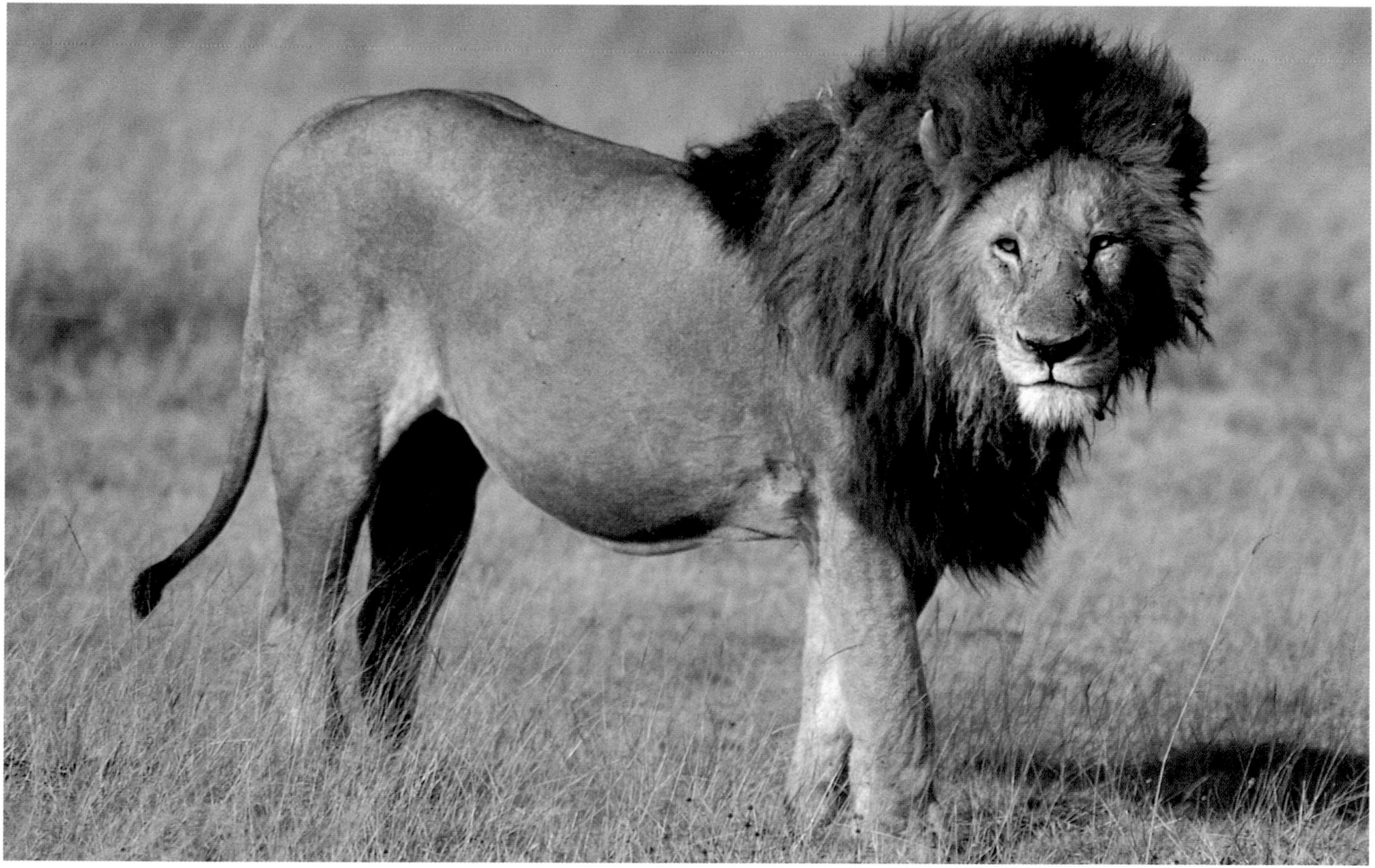

lion

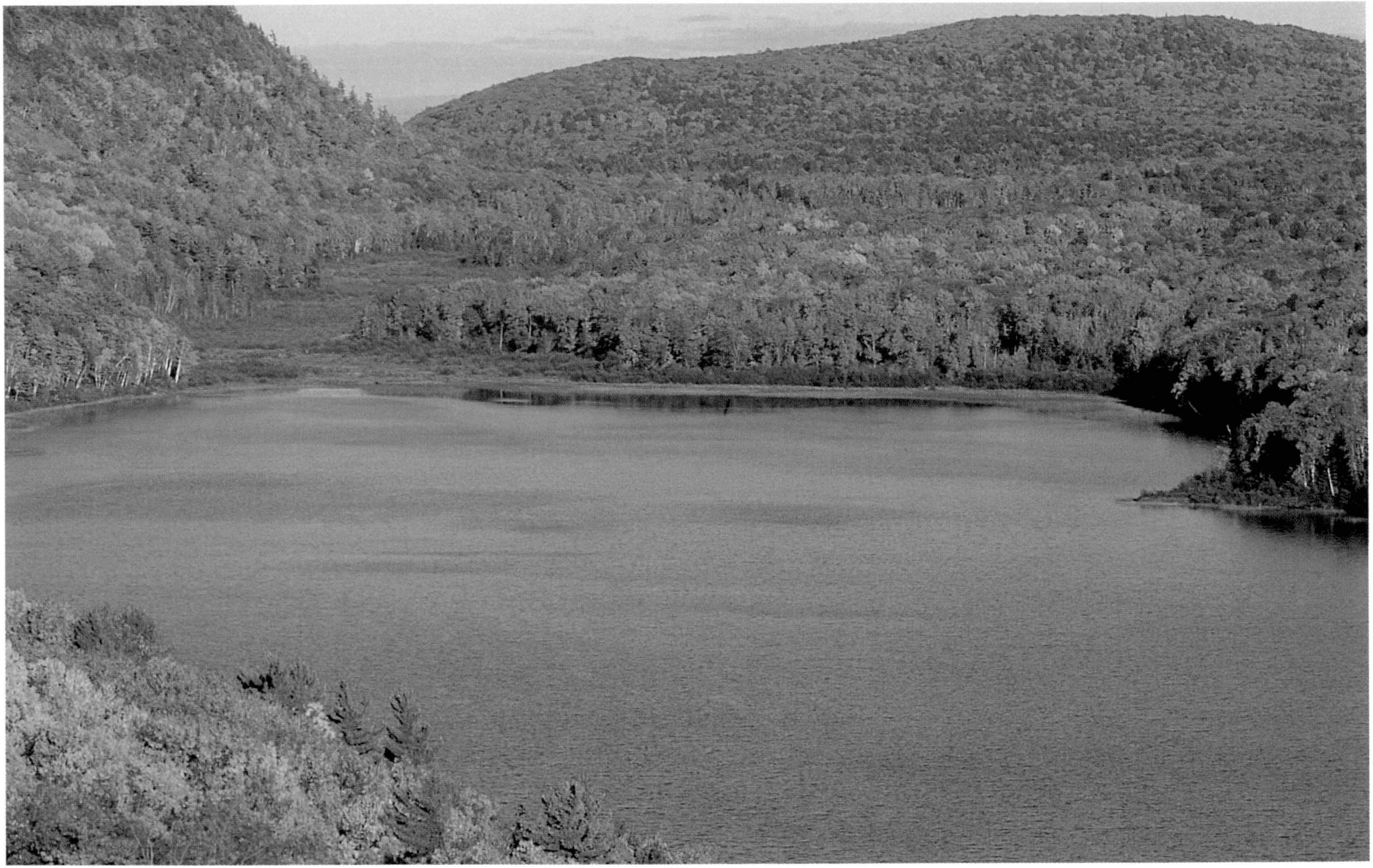

lake

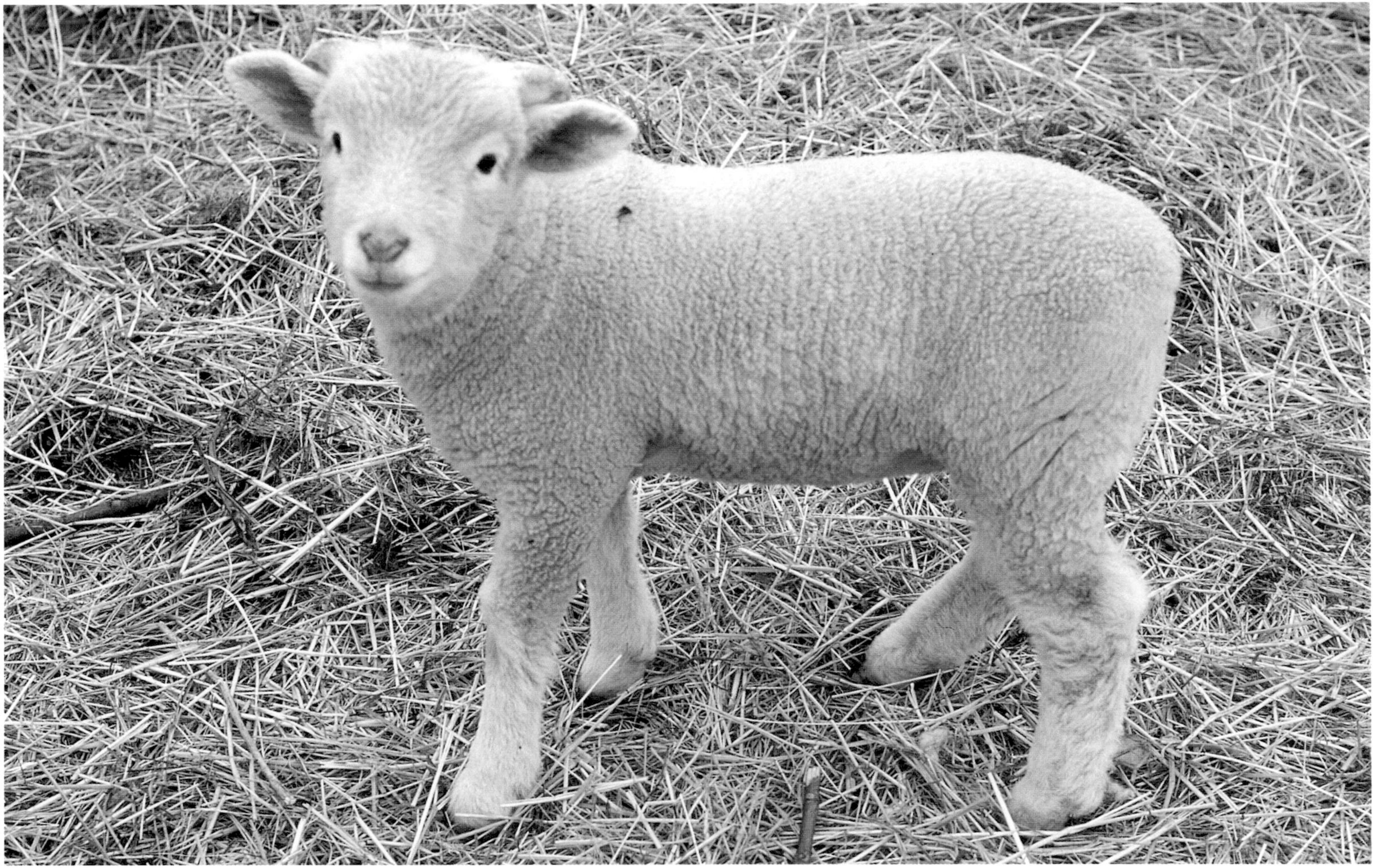

lamb

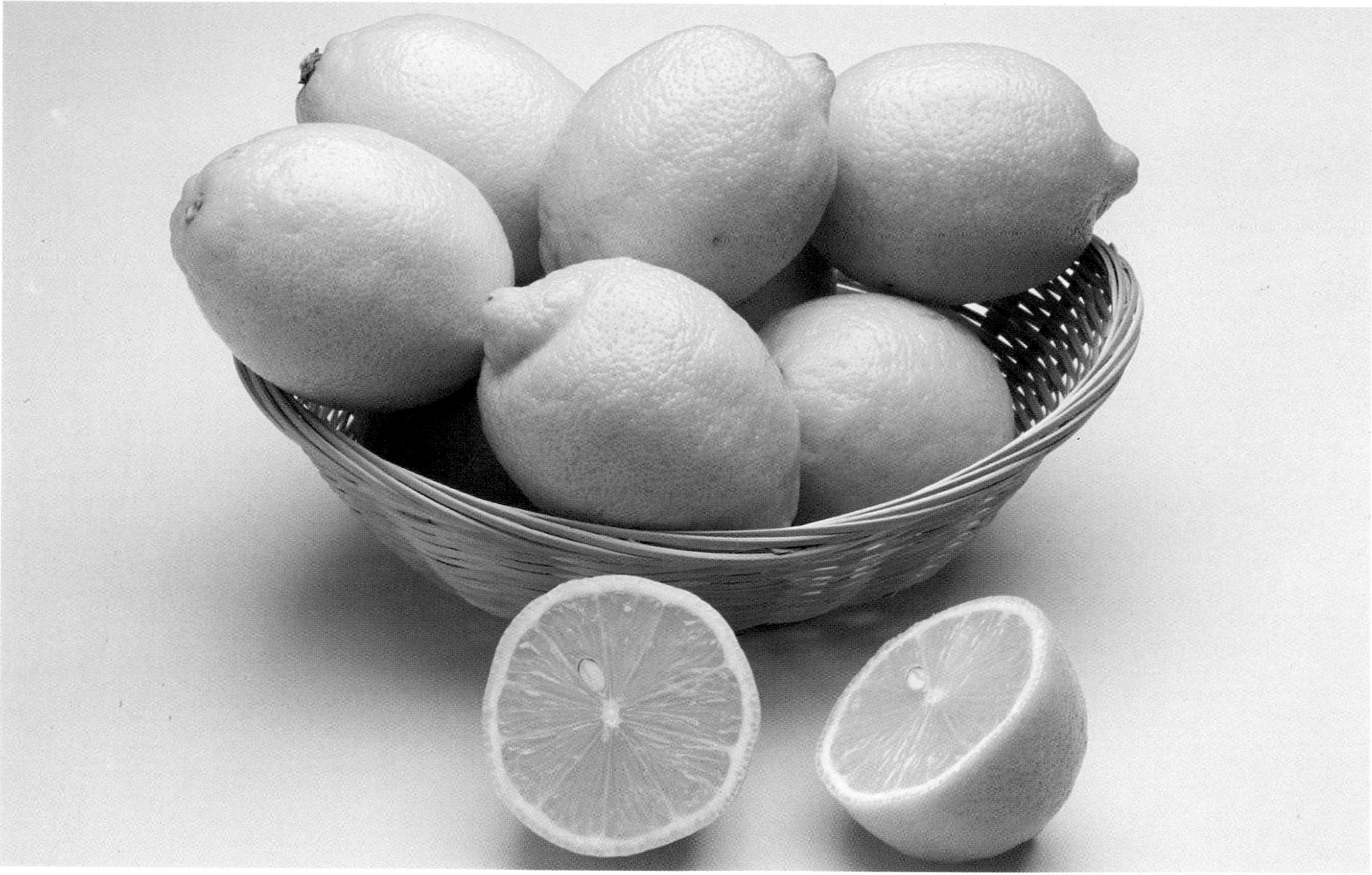

lemons

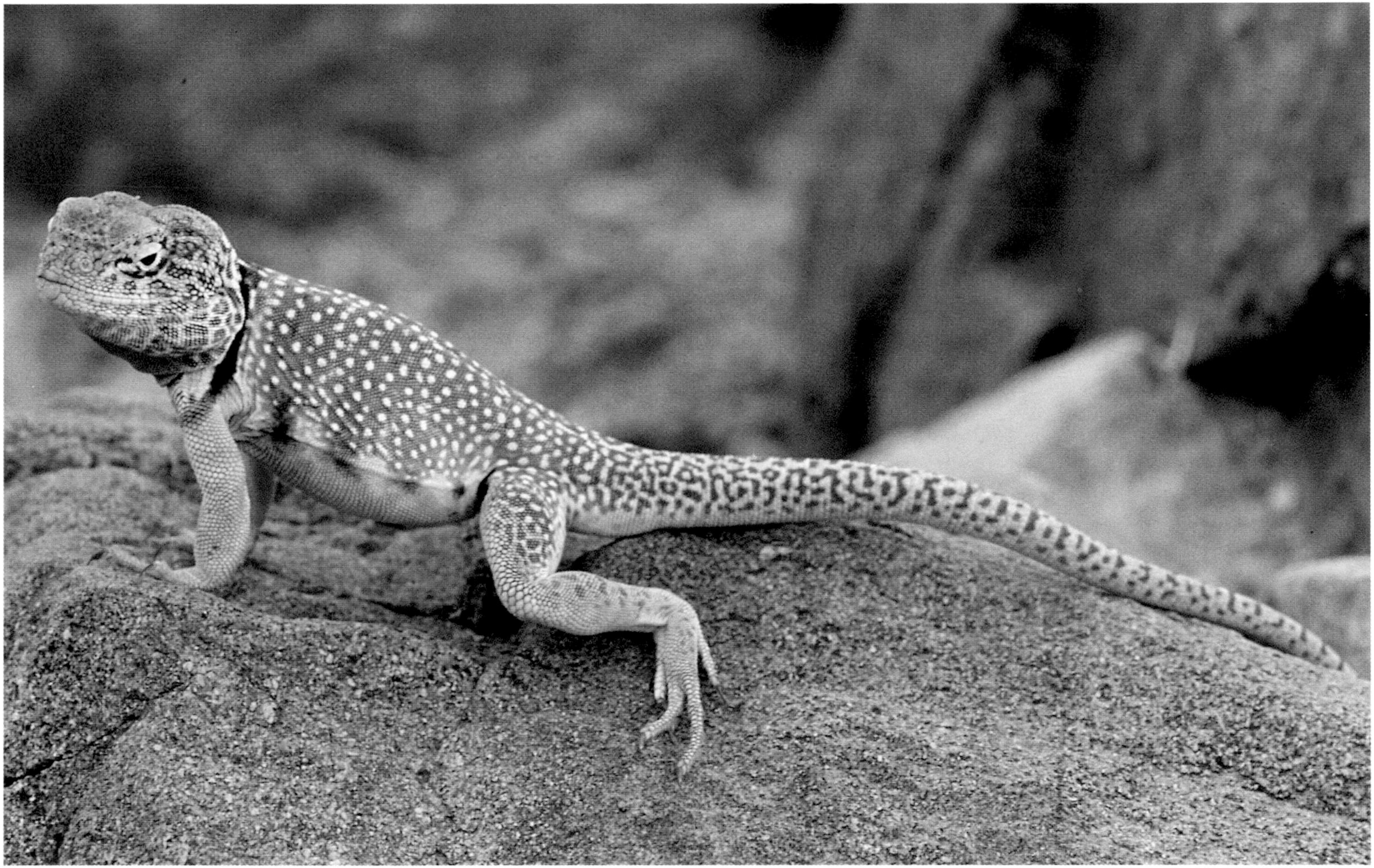

lizard

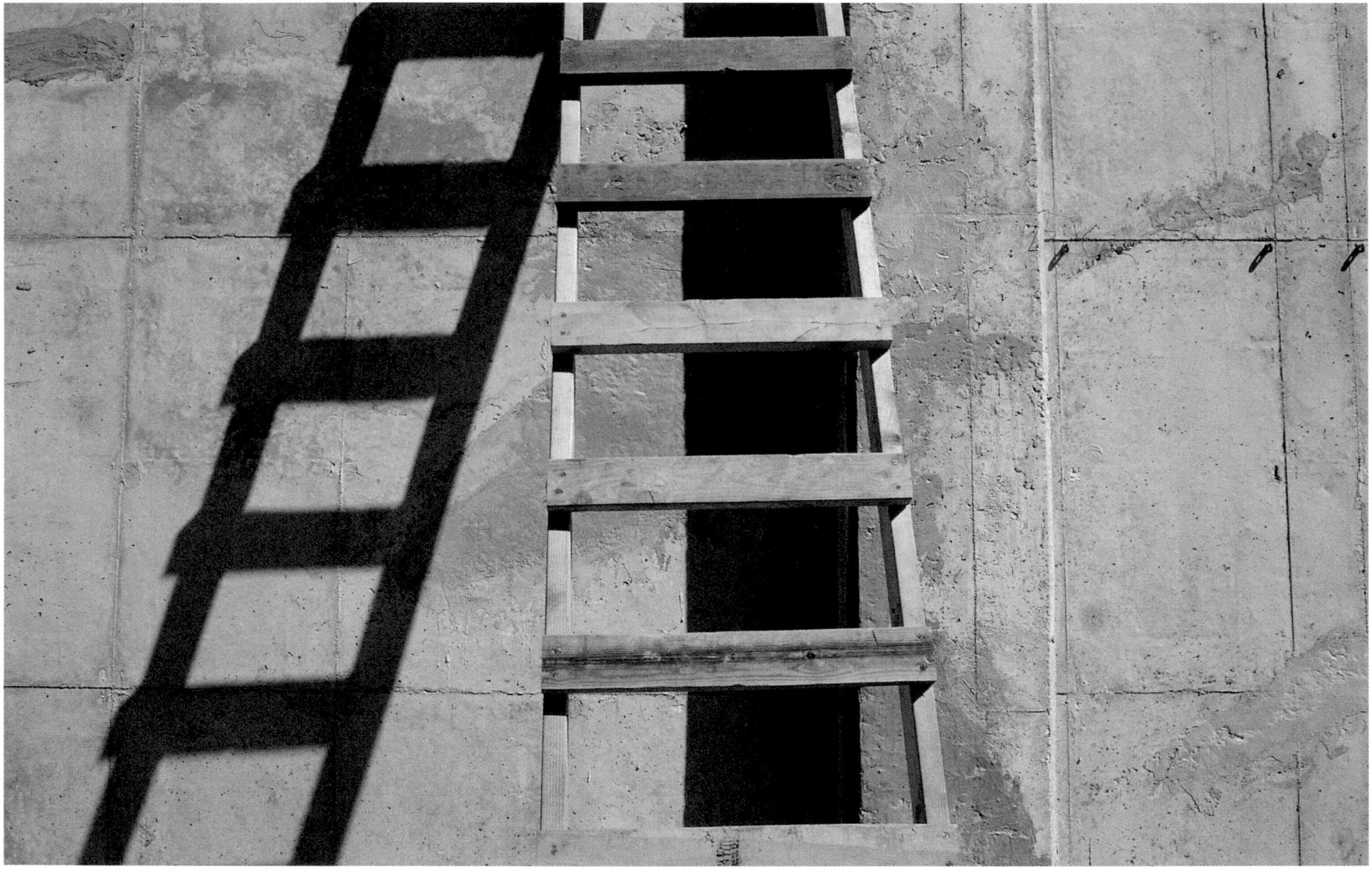

ladder